RAINBOW REMINDERS: What ̄
Cross-Curricular Ac

DON'T STOP! GO THE EXTRA MILE

RAINBOW REMINDERS
What the Colors Tell Us

Anna J. Small Roseboro and Nancy White

Anna J. Small Roseboro, NBCT

Lessons by author, Anna J. Small Roseboro and based on pedagogical approaches to teaching and learning found on websites across the profession devoted to reinforcing knowledge and skills across the content areas.

The pictures and illustrations in **RAINBOW REMINDERS: *What the Colors Tell Us*** are the creative designs of the artist, Nancy White.

Cover graphics
from
https://www.print- print.co.uk/blog/going-the-extra-mile-for-your-customers

ISBN: 9798844060236

Table of Contents

Introduction

More than a story. Use *Rainbow Reminders* as a resource for weeks to expand,

explore and reinforce content and skills.
Parents, teachers, and group leaders can share the original story, store the books, then bring them out weekly for the remainder of the next few months, the course, or school year.

Here are step-by-step guidelines to maximize features in *Rainbow Reminders* as you explore and reinforce knowledge and skills about Creative Writing and also S.T.R.E.A.M. topics of Science, Technology, Reflecting on Religions, Faiths, and Cultures; Energy, Ecology, and English skills (reading, writing, speaking, listening, multi-modal collaborations), Arts, Math, and Music.

There are no "wrong" answers, just incomplete or unsubstantiated ones. So, welcome discussion and comments that encourage students to explain why or how their work fits the activity assignment.

CREATIVE WRITING

Let the words and pictures in
RAINBOW REMINDERS:
What the Color Tell Us
become a springboard from which
readers become writers.

Writing Dialogue

1. Distribute the books and invite students to turn to a page you've preselected with at least one person on the page. Please go over the steps to show them how it could work.

2. Invite students to turn to a different page of their choice with at least one person on it.

3. Now, invite participants to write a dialogue between the two characters: the one you chose and the one on their chosen page.

4. Use the background of the pictures to spur the dialogue. Remember, in dialogue, writers are to change paragraphs each time they change speakers.

Developing Characters

1. Review with students how to develop the personality of a fictional character using the S.T.E.A.L. ELEMENTS. What is the person SAYING about whatever could be happening on the page.? What is the character THINKING about what happened before the picture was taken or drawn or about someone else on the page? What is the EFFECT of this character's actions on others in the book? How does the character A.C.T.? Consider how this character responds when someone says something mean to the character. What does the character LOOK like? Consider gender, physique, clothing, hair, and eyes.

2. Distribute the books and invite students to write their phone numbers on their paper or page.

3. Then circle any five, but different, numbers in that phone number.

4. Next, turn to the five pages that match those numbers. Look carefully at three pages with people on the pages.

5. Now, choose one of those pages and write about that person on the page using the STEAL elements.
6. Invite students who wrote about the person on the same page to meet and share their writing.
7. Invite pairs of students to volunteer to read their different stories. Ask listeners to comment on the accuracy of the STEAL elements even though they are different.

Describing a Place Using Sensory Images

1. Using a *Rainbow Reminders* picture you've chosen, demonstrate how writers can recreate a scene for readers by appealing to the five senses. SIGHT, SOUND, TASTE, TOUCH, and SMELL.
2. Distribute the books. Have five pages in the book pre-selected.
3. Use a randomizer or have students draw numbers to assign students the page from which to write.
4. Invite the students to take the reader into the picture on their "assigned" page and describe what they see in the picture by using appeals to the five senses.
5. Have students who chose the same picture meet and share their writing and blend their images into one group writing. How many images are the same? How many different? How many are surprising but fitting?
6. Invite each group to choose someone to speak for each group. Everyone else turns to the specified page as each group speaker reads their combined description and takes readers INTO the picture.

Plotting A Short Story

1. Review with the students that a short story usually is set in one place and a main character has a problem to solve. Point out the WHO, WHAT, WHEN, WHERE, WHY, and HOW of a story familiar to the students/readers.

2. Distribute the books and invite students to write three numbers between 4-45.

3. Instruct them to turn and look at the words or images on those three pages.

4. Start planning a short story about what they see in the pictures on one of those pages. Include words in their story from one of the three chosen pages.

5. Set the timer for 10-12 minutes and invite them to write whatever comes to mind, including answers to WHO, WHAT, WHEN, WHERE, WHY, AND HOW?

6. Then, when the timer rings, ask them to read what they have written and make at least three changes to make the writing flow more smoothly or complete an unanswered question.

7. Now, turn and talk. Ask them to turn to the person on their left to listen to that person talk about or read the story they started.

8. Then, turn and talk. Please turn to the person on their right, and this time, read or talk about their own story.

9. Finally, invite three students (or more) to have everyone turn to the page about which they wrote and listen to each student tell or read their story.

10. If time permits, invite students to continue writing, adding conflict, a problem the character must solve, and three attempts to solve that problem.

- Try alone
- Accepts help from a friend
- Has to make an internal decision
  (right or wrong, safe or dangerous,
  legal or illegal, obey or disobey,
  keep or lose a friend.)

S.T.R.E.A.M.

in

*RAINBOW REMINDER*S:
What the Colors Tell Use

Science, Technology, Religion, Ecology, Energy, English, Advertisements, Arts, Music, and Math

-S-

SCIENCE

Most of the pictures in *Rainbow Reminders: What the Colors Tell Us* include settings reflecting concepts students learn in science.

Science and Essential Elements

1. Review the concept of the four essential elements and space with students. *Everything in nature is made up of five essential elements:* **earth, water, fire, air, and space.**

2. Distribute the books and invite students to locate pictures that include the four elements and decide whether the way the elements are shown in the picture seem to be "good" or "bad," friendly or dangerous, or any other words that come to mind.

3. Do they find any picture that does not have the elements in view directly, indirectly, literally, or symbolically?

4. SUMMARY: What do you learn about the elements based on how the elements of earth, water, fire, air, and space are shown in this book?

Light Spectrum

1. Distribute the book and invite students to locate at least four different ways the rainbow appears in the book.

2. What do they notice about the arrangement of the colors?

3. Remind them of R.O.Y. G. B.I.V. is a way of remembering the order of colors in the rainbow: Red, Orange, Yellow, Green, Blue, Indigo Violet (or B.I.P.), Blue, Indigo, Purple.

4. Show the students a chart of the primary and secondary colors. Ask them what they notice about the chart and the link to the rainbow. Project for students a short video that shows how white light traveling through a prism or raindrop comes out in colors in the same order as the colors in the rainbow.

(https://www.youtube.com/watch?v=q73VNpFA-0Q)

-T-

TECHNOLOGY

Some of the activities in this booklet invite students to use the technology of their telephones, tablets, computers, or equipment in their science labs.

Technology Helps Tell the Story

1. After you've used *RAINBOW REMINDERS* several times for different purposes, consider inviting students to discover different myths or cultural explanations about the how and why of rainbows.

2. See this website for ten such stories. (Rainbow Myths and Legends | Rainbow Wall)

3. Invite pairs or triads of students to read the same myth and prepare a way to tell that story to the rest of the group the next time the group/class meets.

4. Prepare slides to accompany the story they are telling. Slides should include where students have gotten their information. These can be captions on the page or a slide at the end with the resources consulted. Citing sources is good practice for skills they will need in future courses.

5. Ask students to the natural phenomenon in that location: How important are the four elements: earth, water, fire, and air, to the health and safety of the culture from where the story comes?

6. Ask questions like: What role do those elements play in the telling of that story? Refer to at least three pictures from *RAINBOW REMINDERS*.

7. Invite students to share the Bible story of why humans see a rainbow after the rain. telling of that story? Refer to at least three pictures from *RAINBOW REMINDERS* book.

8. Invite students to share the Bible story of why humans see a rainbow after the rain.

-R-

Reflections and Religions

Activities in this section invite readers to reflect on the words and the pictures, then move beyond them both and consider other cultures. Most cultures have "stories" or "myths" about the origin and significance of rainbows.

Reflecting on Religions

Reflecting on other stories in class or the group, in religious classes like Sunday School, prep for confirmation Bar or Bat Mitzvah, Coming of Age as a Muslim; Koran, Scripture, and Bible stories

1. Distribute the books and invite students to choose anything five pages with words that begin with the same letter as the first letter in their last name.

2. Invite them to look carefully at the words or the pictures and then consider the Bible verses or stories they know.

3. On their pages, write the link between the picture or words and the Bible verse or story they know. For example, what Bible story could go with the words, pictures, or people on at least three of their chosen pages?

4. Guide them to do a museum walk. This means half the students line up around your meeting room. The other half stands in front of one of the people, and that first person shows the page, quotes the scripture, or references the story

and explains in one minute why they are a good match. (Set the time to ring 60 seconds, then ask students to move to the left until half the students have seen the work of the other half of those present.) Now, reverse the process. Have the walkers get their books, stand around the room, and now they become the storytellers.

Reflecting on Other Cultures

1. Before distributing books, invite students to talk about others' terms, emotions, or incidents that readers could connect with the colors of the rainbow.

2. Show them the slide presentation: you can create your own based on the information at this website or email me to borrow one I have created and used with students from middle school through college and adult study groups. ((https://www.thoughtco.com/visual-color-symbolism-chart-by-culture-4062177)

3. After viewing the slides about ways other cultures may view colors, distribute the *Rainbow Reminder* books.

4. Invite students to apply what they have just learned about how other people in cultures view colors and write three to five sentences about four pictures in the book to show how another culture may view the pictures based on what colors mean to them in their culture.

-E-

The activities in this section invite students to explore energy and ecology.

Readers also will find ways to use *RAINBOW REMINDERS: What the Colors Tell Us* as a tool to inspire English Language Learners to use the language to talk and write about the poem and the pictures in this book.

Exploring Ecology

1. Distribute the books after you know students have learned about ecology. Many as early as third grade will have had lessons that as them to consider "the relationships between living organisms, including humans, and their physical environment. Ecology considers organisms at the individual, population, community, ecosystem, and biosphere level."

2. Those in the group will have heard about recycling, safe drinking water, safe places to swim, the benefits and danger of fire, and the danger of climbing and jumping from high above the ground. Invite them to locate pictures or lines in *Rainbow Reminders* that suggest links to ecology in the book.

3. Which pictures suggest harmony with nature?

4. Which shows dissonance with nature?

English Language Learners

Speaking

1. Adapt the lessons to fit the language acquisition skills your children or students currently have. For example, once you have taught a significant number of nouns, verbs, and adjectives, use *RAINBOW REMINDERS* to inspire students to use the words they are learning.

2. Invite them to turn to a page you choose. Could be the page number of the date you do the activity.

3. Point to details on that page and speak or write using the words they are learning.

4. Or invite them to use their tablets or cell phones to look up the English words for what they see on the page.

5. Invite them to speak aloud in complete sentences to have a conversation about the pictures on that page using the words and verb forms they are learning.

English Language Learners

Writing

1. Invite students to turn to a page in *RAINBOW REMINDERS* that has more than one person on it. Have each student in a pair or triad choose to be one of those persons.

2. Then, invite the students first to speak a dialogue of three to five exchanges. Each person say something. The next person answers or asks a question. Continue so each person speaks three to five times.

3. If they are learning adjectives, include them in their speaking and writing. For example, "See. The yellow butterfly sits on the big flower."

4. If those in the group are learning prepositions, use them to show the location of things in the pictures.

5. Then, ask the speakers write that dialogue using the syntax and punctuation they are learning.

-A-

The activities in this section invite readers to consider the art used in advertisements and the ways that different colors may create mood or tones based on the culture of the observer.

RAINBOW REMINDERS includes lots of art, but readers do not have to limit themselves to the art in this book. They can create their own based on the words in the poem, and the thinking evoked by the art.

ART in Advertising

1. Show students five or ten advertisements for items familiar to those in your group.
2. Invite students to think, go online and find five advertisements for similar products, or just close their eyes and visualize ads they have seen in magazines, on television, on websites, and on billboards.
3. What colors appear most in advertisements in the United States?
4. Ask, "Why do you think the same colors are used so often?"
5. How might viewers from different cultures view or make meaning from the pictures?
6. Invite students to meet in pairs or triads and write their combined thoughts about two different advertisements.

Artists' Use of Colors

1. Distribute the RAINBOW REMINDERS and invite students who are just beginning to read, but know their colors to find five pictures with fewer than five colors.

2. Then, four pages with more than ten different colors.

3. Consider posting a list of colors so students can practice their reading and writing. For younger students, you could have a chart with the colors and the word next to the colors to help students make associations.

4. Encourage to note the colors that appear in most of the pictures.

5. Ask the students if they see more PRIMARY colors or SECONDARY COLORS.

6. Invite them to consider the reasons many artists use specific colors together.

Artists in Your Group

1. Invite those in your group to select words from the *RAINBOW REMINDERS'* pages and draw pictures to illustrate those words.

2. Encourage those in your group to create their own ROY G. BIV books with a least one page for each color in the rainbow (red, orange, yellow, green, blue, indigo, violet). Consider pairs and triads so students can "teach" each other as they prepare their booklets or slide presentations.

3. Draw, paint, or make collages to go with what you've written. Feel free to be realistic or abstract.

4. Ask them to consider the colors as key elements in the story, the colors of clothing, furniture, toys, cars, or something else in their story. What mood or tone is set by the colors that dominate their story?

5. Invite them to share their stories with three people outside of their household.

6. Share with family or classmates.

-M-

MUSIC and MATH

Most of the pictures in *Rainbow Reminders: What the Colors Tell Us* evoke emotions as does music.

There always are seven colors in the rainbow. Invite students to use their understanding of math: recognizing numbers and doing activities that may ask them to count images in pictures, choose particular page numbers for activities, or learn how to write their birth dates in numbers.

MATH AND WORDS

Math Practice and Word Recognition for Students Learning to Read English

1. Distribute the *RAINBOW REMINDERS* book.
2. Invite students to find at least three words that begin with the same letter as the child's first and last names.
3. Write the letters of their name in a column down the right side of the paper.
4. Then, find one word for each letter in their first and last name. Copy each word onto the paper next to the letter.
5. Find different words if the name has the same letter more than once.
6. Who in the group has the most different words for the different letters? (For example, my name has two of the letter A. I must find two different words that begin with A.)
7. Now, write or tell a story that uses those words.

More Math for Young Ones

BIRTHDATES IN NUMBERS

1. The goal is to learn about writing dates as numbers, practice addition, and experience close viewing of artwork.
2. Have students write their birth dates using numbers for the month and day. (My son's birthday is June 28. So, is number number would be $7 + 28 = 35$.)
3. Add those numbers the numbers that match the birthday.
4. Distribute the RAINBOW REMINDERS book.
5. Match the sum of those numbers to a page in *Rainbow Reminders.*
6. Make a list of the details they notice on that page. Invite them to look at words and images on the left and right side pages. Notice details on both pages. Choose words.
7. Include the words on that page in the story that tell or write.
8. Consider writing a group or class story using two words offered by each participant.

MUSIC AND EMOTIONS
Collaborating with Peers

1. Distribute *RAINBOW REMINDERS* and invite students to consider the writing in the poem as it relates to the pictures on which the writing appears.
2. What colors suggest what moods? Or express specific emotions? (Consider projecting colorless emojis showing different emotions. Invite pairs or triads to choose colors for ten emojis. Then explain the color and suggest popular music to go with the colors.)
3. Then invite students to work in pairs or triads to create their slide presentation using the words from the book, but locating, copying, and pasting their chosen pictures to illustrate the poem with different pictures.
4. Invite one student to find three minutes of music to play while the ir group pictures are showing. No words. Just pictures and music. (Consider public domain music on sites like bensound.com.)
5. Consider inserting mp3 files into PowerPoint or Google Slides.
6. Reserve fifteen minutes to play the "slide shows" of students' pictures and music.

Exploring *RAINBOW REMINDERS* with Senior Citizens

1. Distribute the RAINBOW REMINDER book or show slides of the e-book.
2. Invite participants to share stories of their literal and metaphorical experiences before, during, and after the rain.
3. Plan future gatherings where participants are invited do some of the activities described here in the handbook of activities.
4. If the technology for online searches is not easily accessible, provide paper and colored pencils for participants to sketch, draw and diagram their responses, using appropriate colors to reflect the setting, situations, events, and emotions.
5. Invite participants to share their writing and drawing.
6. Encourage participants to take photos of their work and share with family and friends.
7. Encourage participants to purchase books as gifts for family members.

About the Author

Anna J. Small Roseboro, a National Board-Certified Teacher has over four decades of experience teaching in public and private schools, mentoring early career educators, and facilitating leadership institutes. She has tutored adult English Language Learners through the Literacy Center of West Michigan. She was awarded Distinguished Service Awards by the California Association of Teachers of English and the National Council of Teachers of English.

https://ajsmallroseboro.wordpress.com

Made in the USA
Columbia, SC
13 November 2022

71078263R00024